Tomatoes
to Ketchup

by Lisa M. Herrington

Content Consultant
J. Peter Clark, Ph.D., P.E., Consultant to the Process Industries

Reading Consultant
Jeanne Clidas, Ph.D.

Children's Press®
An Imprint of Scholastic Inc.
New York Toronto London Auckland Sydney
Mexico City New Delhi Hong Kong
Danbury, Connecticut

Cataloging-in-Publication Data is available from the Library of Congress

ISBN 978-0-531-24743-3 (lib. bdg.)
ISBN 978-0-531-24709-9 (pbk.)

Produced by Spooky Cheetah Press

Printed in China 62

SCHOLASTIC, CHILDREN'S PRESS, ROOKIE READ-ABOUT®, and associated logos are trademarks and/or registered trademarks of Scholastic Inc.

1 2 3 4 5 6 7 8 9 10 R 22 21 20 19 18 17 16 15 14 13

Photographs © 2013: age fotostock: 15 (David Thurber), 8 (Dennis MacDonald); AP Images/Keith Srakocic: 27, 30 bottom; Getty Images/Ed Darack: cover top right, 23, 30 center bottom; Courtesy of Heinz: 24, 30 second from bottom, 31 center top; iStockphoto/Floortje: 3 top; Media Bakery: cover top center, 20, 30 center top (Mark/Audrey Gibson), 4; PhotoEdit: 31 bottom (Mark Richards), 19 (Michael Newman); Shutterstock, Inc.: cover top left, 7, 30 top (Anna Jurkovska), 12 (Gorilla), 16, 30 second from top (Karin Hildebrand Lau), 3 bottom, 31 center bottom (Peter Zijlstra), 11 (REDAV); Thinkstock: 28 (Christopher Robbins), cover bottom (Hemera), 31 top (iStockphoto).

Table of Contents

Ketchup adds taste to food.

4

It Starts with a Seed

Nearly every American home has ketchup in it. Ketchup is a thick, red sauce. Find out how it is made.

Ketchup comes from tomatoes.

Bright red tomatoes are the most important ingredient in ketchup.

All tomatoes grow from seeds. The seeds are planted in the ground.

Workers plant seeds on a huge tomato farm.

Tomato plants need plenty of sunshine and water to grow.

Then the tomatoes grow on vines.

Many people think tomatoes are vegetables. Scientists say a tomato is a fruit because it has seeds.

Ripe and Ready!

Some seeds grow into tomatoes that people pick and put in salads.

This girl is picking tomatoes in her family's garden.

13

Other seeds grow into tomatoes that will be used for ketchup. Farmers use machines to pick **ripe** ketchup tomatoes.

On large farms, harvesting machines are used to pick the tomatoes.

From Farm to Factory

The tomatoes are loaded onto trucks. A standard tomato truck can hold about 300,000 tomatoes.

The trucks take the tomatoes to ketchup **factories**.

Tomatoes that are used for ketchup have thick skins. That keeps them from getting damaged on the truck.

382A

LF2901

At the factory, machines wash and cut the tomatoes. They also remove the seeds and skin.

A moving belt carries tomatoes underneath sprayers on the washing machine.

The tomatoes are cooked. They turn into a thick **paste**.

As the tomatoes cook, they lose water. That makes them thicken into paste.

Vinegar, sweeteners, salt, and spices are added to the paste. That is what gives ketchup its taste.

If ketchup were made with only tomatoes, it would taste much different!

Ready to Eat

The ketchup flows through screens. The screens catch any seeds or skins that are left. Then the ketchup is put into bottles.

The ketchup is ready to eat! What do you like to put ketchup on?

FUN FACT!

Americans use about three bottles of ketchup per person each year.

Making Ketchup
Step by Step

 1. The tomatoes are picked.

 2. Trucks take the tomatoes to factories.

 3. The tomatoes are washed and cut.

 4. The tomatoes are cooked into a thick paste.

 5. Sugar, salt, and other things are added.

 6. The ketchup is put into containers.

Glossary

factories (FAK-tuh-rees): buildings where things are made

paste (payst): a thick, creamy mixture

ripe (ripe): ready to be harvested, picked, or eaten

vinegar (VIN-uh-gur): a sour liquid used to flavor and preserve some foods

Index

Facts for Now

Visit this Scholastic Web site for more information on
how ketchup is made:
www.factsfornow.scholastic.com
Enter the keyword **Ketchup**

About the Author

Lisa M. Herrington writes books and magazine articles for kids. She lives in Trumbull, Connecticut, with her husband and daughter. You can often find her topping her scrambled eggs with ketchup!

8/19 27 2/19